The Little Book of Corporate Lies

(What They Say . . .
*What They **Really** Mean*)

By

BRUCE T. SMITH

LAURA GOECKE BURNS

MICHAEL BURNS

CCC PUBLICATIONS

Published by

CCC Publications
1111 Rancho Conejo Blvd.
Suites 411 & 412
Newbury Park, CA 91320

Manufactured in the United States of America

Cover/Interior production by Oasis Graphics

ISBN: 0-57644-024-9

If your local U.S. bookstore is out of stock, copies of
this book may be obtained by mailing check or
money order for $6.95 per book (plus $2.50 to cover
postage and handling) to:
CCC Publications; 111 Rancho Conejo Blvd.;
Suites 411 & 412; Newbury Park, CA 91320

Pre-publication Edition – 10/96

Foreword...

This book started out as therapy.

JUST LIKE YOU, we were caught up like rats in the corporate maze of American business, constantly bombarded with an endless stream of meaningless platitudes, mind-numbing bromides and insulting clichés as we watched our jobs (and our lives) get downsized, flattened, outsourced and strategized.

Not long after we'd endured yet another overweight, balding, mid-level manager tell us that all our pay-raises were frozen until morale improved – we decided it was time for the rats to redesign the maze. That's when we started collecting the examples you'll find in the pages of this humble book. We quickly discovered our efforts therapeutic: for rather than wincing at corporate America's senseless verbiage, we started laughing! And, once we started laughing a lot we decided to share the fun (and irony) with you.

The best part is that our corporate bosses had no idea they made such terrific "straight men." (But then, antacid junkies generally have no sense of the world around them, do they?)

So, if you've heard a good one from the world of corporate babble – send it to us, together with your translation, at CorpSpeak@AOL.COM. We'll pick the very best entry and OUR PUBLISHERS will send you a check for $100.00. Best of all, we'll credit you with the idea in "The Little Book of Corporate Lies: Volume II" – That is if OUR PUBLISHERS decide to print a second volume.

In the meantime, keep laughing. It beats the hell out of the alternatives.

Bruce, Laura and Mike

WHAT THEY SAY . . .

I am going to
empower you.

* * *

WHAT THEY
REALLY MEAN . . .

*Don't even think of
making a decision
without my approval.*

We are going to
reengineer for a more
efficient operation

* * *

*MOST of you are
going to lose your
jobs.*

We are going to strategically downsize.

* * *

The REST of you are going to lose your jobs.

We are all part of a team and YOU need to support this project.

* * *

I made a stupid mistake and YOU'RE stuck with it.

I sense you're not a
part of the team.

* * *

*If you don't admit
responsibility for my
mistake, you're fired.*

We are instituting a
bonus incentive
program to give you a
stake in the
company's future.

* * *

***Kiss your annual
raise goodbye!***

We feel you are just
not management
material.

* * *

*You have too much
common sense and
integrity.*

We have a 40-hour
work week here.

* * *

*That's not counting
nights, weekends and
holidays, of course.*

If you will stick with me through this transition, there will be plenty of opportunities for you as the company grows.

* * *

You're going nowhere fast, but I need you to do the dog work until I throw you out like yesterday's garbage.

We want you to adopt
our corporate values.

* * *

*I want you to suck up
to me more.*

We can create some efficiencies.

* * *

You'll be working lots of unpaid overtime.

We're implementing a paradigm shift.

* * *

We're going to do what we've always done, but now we're going to call it something different.

We're going to maximize our office environment.

* * *

You don't mind subdividing your cubicle, do you?

Please bring your
wife.

* * *

*And make sure she
wears that short,
little black cocktail
dress.*

Please bring your
husband.

* * *

*I can talk about
football with HIM!*

Promotion opportunities for women here are not limited by a glass ceiling.

* * *

That's because OUR ceiling is made out of lead!

We are firmly
committed to
affirmative action.

* * *

*We have several
openings on our
janitorial staff.*

Are you p.c. literate?

* * *

We don't have the money for a secretarial staff.

We have concluded
our downsizing
initiative and we're
now entering a period
of managed growth.

* * *

*You're lucky you still
have a job, but don't
EVEN think of
asking for a raise.*

We are eliminating your position, but we have enrolled you in an outplacement seminar to ease your transition to a new career.

* * *

You'll learn new phrases like: "You want fries with that?"

We trust our employees to do their jobs and not waste company time on personal matters.

* * *

We're monitoring your phone, e-mail and correspondence to find a reason to can you and spread fear among your fellow employees.

We're going to create a sustainable marketing concept that integrates our target markets with distribution channels and internal service delivery capabilities.

* * *

Miss this month's sales quota and you'll be stacking boxes in the basement.

We will approach our expense-reduction strategy around the concept of reengineering the work through the appropriate application of technology.

* * *

You've been replaced by a computer.

Please, feel free to
use my voice mail.

* * *

*That way, I can
delete and ignore
your call.*

We're going to flatten our corporate structure.

* * *

We're going to steamroller YOUR department.

We have created a
TOTAL QUALITY
environment.

* * *

*We have a committee
to check on our
committees that
report to other
committees to ensure
nothing changes.*

Jane opted for early retirement.

* * *

Jane was fired.

We have hired the finest legal mind in the country to solve this problem.

* * *

She's my sister-in-law.

We offer a competitive health care package.

* * *

We hope you don't mind having your child's appendix taken out by a veterinarian.

Send me an e-mail with the details. I'll make a copy for the file.

* * *

I can blame YOU when it hits the fan around here.

Your proposals are
innovative and bold.

* * *

*I'm going to present
YOUR proposals to
the CEO as MY
proposals.*

I really like your drive.

* * *

Show me up one more time in front of the CEO and I'll car-bomb you.

He has style.

* * *

His suit is more expensive than yours and so is his car AND he lets me win at tennis.

I have an open door policy.

* * *

So, turn around and walk out.

We need a total team
effort from all of you.

* * *

*If my pet project
fails, you're all
history.*

We are convinced this is a realistic budget.

* * *

Actually, I pulled these figures out of my ass.

Our division did not
meet budget this
quarter.

* * *

*We didn't make
enough money to
cover my bonus —
so you need to fire
more employees.*

We need to focus on
team building.

* * *

*I want hang out with
you guys so you don't
talk about me.*

Accounting has
implemented an
aggressive cost-
savings initiative.

* * *

*You have to supply
your own secretary,
computer, and desk.*

The executives on the
enterprise team are
meeting to discuss
"corporate strategy".

* * *

*Their tee time is at
4:00 p.m.*

Jane, of course I'm deeply committed to sexual equality in the workplace.

* * *

OK. YOU get to pick the motel next time...

Human Resources is screening several top candidates from outside the company.

* * *

You didn't REALLY believe us when we said we'd "promote from within," did you?

Due to compelling economic forces, it is with deep regret the board announces the following layoffs....

* * *

It is with extreme pleasure the board has voted itself a bonus.

We are implementing
a time-management
study.

* * *

*We are installing
surveillance cameras
in the bathrooms.*

We vision ourselves
as a corporate family.

* * *

*Dysfunctional,
incestuous, but a
family nonetheless.*

The board is confident this merger is in the very best interests of the stockholders.

* * *

The board is equally confident this merger is in the very worst interests of its employees.

This hostile takeover is not in the best interests of our stockholders and employees.

* * *

We officers and board members haven't been offered enough money to sell your jobs down the river...YET!

We are all part of the Corporate TEAM!

* * *

We're about to hit you up for the CEO's favorite charity.

Your executive management team certainly understands your anxiety the recent layoffs have caused.

* * *

Your executive management team will be vacationing in Tahiti until things cool off.

Our reengineering
efforts are not a
backhanded approach
to cutting staff.

* * *

*Our efforts are
actually an open-
handed, slap-in-
the-face!!*

We've retained a consulting firm to plan the festivities for the corporate anniversary.

* * *

...and you wonder why you haven't had a raise in two years.

We have completed our work on the new, state-of-the-art file retrieval system.

* * *

We laid off the entire clerical staff. You'll now be searching for the files yourselves.

I have studied your proposal in depth.

* * *

I don't have a clue what you're talking about.

I want YOU to present MY proposal to the board....

* * *

I don't want to take the blame when the board rejects the idea.

These staff reductions are necessary so we can compete aggressively in the global marketplace!

* * *

You're being transferred to Tijuana.

We have installed an automated phone system to provide efficient service to our customers.

* * *

We'll let Voice Mail talk to them...so we don't have to be bothered with their complaints.

We are managing change.

* * *

We are changing managers.

In these challenging
economic times we
are looking to do
MORE with LESS!

* * *

*We want MORE of
your blood and you'll
get LESS vacation.*

I'm behind you 100%

* * *

If you do one more thing I don't like, you're toast.

With authority comes responsibly.

* * *

You don't really have any authority...but you'll get all the blame.

We want to provide "value added" services to our customers.

* * *

That is for customers who happen to be shareholders!

We want to sell a
quality product at a
reasonable price.

* * *

*We want to sell an
inferior product and
an outrageous price.*

The company and Mr. Jones reached an amicable parting.

* * *

The company paid Mr. Jones a boatload of cash after he filed suit.

You did an
EXCELLENT job
this year!

* * *

*But NOT excellent
enough for a raise.*

We need to control
expenses.

* * *

*Your salary is
frozen...and we
expect you to sprout
another ulcer
working unpaid
overtime... again.*

We have retained the most prestigious consulting firm in America to help us vision our strategic plan....

* * *

...and the fee we pay THEM is equal to YOUR pay cut.

We're a "family friendly" company.

* * *

Don't worry if you get pregnant. After you lose your job, you'll have plenty of time to spend with your kids.

You have an attitude
problem.

* * *

*I don't like it when
you point out my
mistakes.*

You need to be more productive.

* * *

You can get a lot more work done during your additional midnight to 5:00 am shift.

I sense you are not quite ready for additional responsibilities.

* * *

In order to promote my crony ahead of you, I had to invent a vague and meaningless criticism on your evaluation form.

We are not raising employee pay this year in an effort to bring our salaries in line with other companies.

* * *

Other companies in Bangladesh, that is.

You are, without a doubt, the smartest person in the department. I really need you...but John is getting the promotion.

* * *

John sucks up to me more than you do.

We need a well-rounded employee who balances work and family.

* * *

You didn't want more than one unpaid hour to visit your sick child in the hospital, did you?

We hired a consultant to help us cut our travel expenses.

* * *

She recommends you stay with your ex in-laws during your next trip to Cleveland.

We really hated to let you go, but your position has been eliminated.

* * *

I've wanted to dump you for years - but couldn't come up with a good enough reason.

We need to make
decisions at the
LOWEST operational
levels.

* * *

*God knows we
wouldn't want to
make any decisions
at the HIGHEST
operational levels.*

We've been a leader
in equal opportunities
for women. Why,
we've had a female
VP for over a decade.

* * *

**And we're still
paying her what she
earned in 1982.**

We are aggressively pursuing the European market.

* * *

The CEO's wife wants to spend three weeks in Paris this summer.

This newly created
cost-savings position
is unique to the
industry.

* * *

***Not EVERY
company has a toilet-
paper monitor.***

I really went to bat
for you on that issue.
But the board
outvoted me.

* * *

*You don't seriously
think I risked MY job
for you, do you?*

This is for the good of
the company.

* * *

*This sucks the big
one for YOU.*

Due to diminished cost-benefit efficiency, we're eliminating the company car program.

* * *

The CEO's last three DWI's sent our insurance premium through the roof.

We have to create
processes which are:
a) more user friendly
for the customer,
b) less costly and,
c) more efficient for us.

* * *

*Therefore, you will: a)
learn to type, b) fire your
secretary and, c) don't
even think of asking for
a day off.*

During this critical phase of reengineering, you may have to take on new or different responsibilities or learn new job skills.

* * *

Actually, serving as a caddy for the CEO can have its own rewards.

We'll have a short corporate strategy session right after lunch.

* * *

Call your sitters, you won't be home for dinner.

As your CEO, I am reducing the prospects for FUTURE layoffs.

* * *

So, you're out RIGHT NOW!

Change of this
magnitude is neither
comfortable nor easy.

* * *

*Unless you're an
executive with a
no-cut contract.*

We're switching to a managed health care program.

* * *

If you manage to stay healthy, you'll be able to afford aspirin.

We have a new cost-effective dental plan.

* * *

You'll notice a floss recycling bin has been placed in the lunchroom.

We are going to MAXIMIZE our output by MINIMIZING our costs.

* * *

Actually we're going to MINIMIZE your salary and MAXIMIZE your unpaid overtime.

We are an equal opportunity employer, committed to racial diversity in our workforce.

* * *

We're expecting ANOTHER truckload of illegal aliens tonight.

We are aggressively seeking new blood and fresh ideas for the 21st century.

* * *

We'll hire recent college grads cheaply and "outplace" them before their 401K plans vest.

We're spending too much time in unproductive meetings.

* * *

Let's schedule a conference to discuss the problem.

A decision this vital
to the company must
be made by senior
management.

* * *

*Will that be red or
white wine with
dinner?*

We must maximize
our use of technology
to regain our
competitive edge.

* * *

*We're going to add
computers and
eliminate people.*

The company encourages all employees to speak freely with any company officer about complaints with no fear of reprisal.

* * *

Unless your complaint is about a company officer, in which case you'll be shot.

We must develop
strategic alternatives
by identifying our
sources of input.

* * *

*We might actually
read an employee
suggestion for a
change.*

In these tough economic times, we must improve the public image our corporation projects.

* * *

We're buying a fleet of Mercedes-Benz for the corporate officers.

I urge you to join me
in supporting this
important initiative.

* * *

*Support my program
or die.*

By proactively evaluating and changing processes and roles now, we will greatly reduce the chance of future layoffs.

* * *

Many of you will enjoy the challenges the mail room has to offer.

Affirmative steps will be taken to increase representation of minorities and women at all organizational levels.

* * *

Unfortunately, we can't find any disabled Aleutian women veterans to serve on our board.

ALL employees will
be compensated on
the principle of equal
pay for equal work.

* * *

*You'll ALL be paid
like migrant farm
workers.*

Outsourcing doesn't necessarily mean layoffs.

* * *

And the Pope doesn't necessarily have to be Catholic, either.

In these competitive
economic times, we'll
all have to tighten our
belts.

* * *

*Your choices are
these: either eat OR
pay your rent.*

In our continuing efforts to cut expenses and make this company more profitable, there will be NO SACRED COWS!

* * *

Except, of course, country club memberships for corporate officers.

This is, BY NO MEANS, a personal reflection upon you or your abilities.

* * *

This is, ABSOLUTELY, a personal reflection upon you and your abilities.

Your proud and honored, long-tenure of outstanding service to this company...

* * *

...could cost us a ton of money in pension pay-outs. You're fired.

A representative from Human Resources is always available to assist you with any problem you encounter in the work environment.

* * *

Our snitches in Human Resources will let us know if you are a team player or not.

The company is committed to the treatment of all employees in a fair, respectful and dignified manner.

* * *

Just kidding.

On business, male and female employees must exercise discretion and awareness that their private conduct reflects on our corporate image.

* * *

Before returning from a business trip, male employees are reminded to remove panties and brassieres from their briefcases.

If you have questions regarding corporate personnel policy, please consult the employee handbook....

* * *

...our lawyers have assured us the handbook contains nothing helpful to you.

We do not have sufficient resources to implement your project.

* * *

We have laid off so many people that we can't do any meaningful work.

Air travel
arrangements will be
made with
ECONOMY in mind.

* * *

*Employees will book
all future flights on
Value Jet.*

We provide a generous per diem for our employees on business travel.

* * *

You'll be eating peanuts and a soda for breakfast. AND lunch.

We are pleased to implement a "casual day" for our company.

* * *

You'll have to purchase an expensive business casual wardrobe. (Non deductible, of course.)

Our efficiency consultants have identified low-value activities that can be eliminated to free up our employees for more meaningful and productive efforts.

* * *

Such as sleeping, eating, procreating...

Innovative ideas are critical to making positive change happen.

$$* \quad * \quad *$$

As long as they don't involve changes in MY department.

We must think
"outside the box".

* * *

*Your job description
now includes "spying
on the competition."*

Your senior
management team is
committed to
corporate loyalty....

* * *

*the same way a
shark is loyal to a
feeding tuna.*

We are setting goals
that are challenging,
yet attainable.

* * *

**We are setting
unrealistic goals so
we can demote you
when you don't
meet them.**

We must look beyond cost in order to find the best alternative.

* * *

ALWAYS pick the cheapest alternative.

Senior m
will now
quickly t
employ

ma

cor

...by
emplo
box
pa

....in
sha
bl

TITLES BY CCC PUBLICATIONS

Retail $4.99
"?" book
POSITIVELY PREGNANT
WHY MEN ARE CLUELESS
CAN SEX IMPROVE YOUR GOLF?
THE COMPLETE BOOGER BOOK
FLYING FUNNIES
MARITAL BLISS & OXYMORONS
THE VERY VERY SEXY ADULT DOT-TO-DOT BOOK
THE DEFINITIVE FART BOOK
THE COMPLETE WIMP'S GUIDE TO SEX
THE CAT OWNER'S SHAPE UP MANUAL
PMS CRAZED: TOUCH ME AND I'LL KILL YOU!
RETIRED: LET THE GAMES BEGIN
THE OFFICE FROM HELL
FOOD & SEX
FITNESS FANATICS
YOUNGER MEN ARE BETTER THAN RETIN-A
BUT OSSIFER, IT'S NOT MY FAULT

Retail $4.95
YOU KNOW YOU'RE AN OLD FART WHEN...
1001 WAYS TO PROCRASTINATE
HORMONES FROM HELL II
SHARING THE ROAD WITH IDIOTS
THE GREATEST ANSWERING MACHINE MESSAGES OF ALL TIME
WHAT DO WE DO NOW?? (A Guide For New Parents)
HOW TO TALK YOU WAY OUT OF A TRAFFIC TICKET
THE BOTTOM HALF (How To Spot Incompetent Professionals)
LIFE'S MOST EMBARRASSING MOMENTS
HOW TO ENTERTAIN PEOPLE YOU HATE
YOUR GUIDE TO CORPORATE SURVIVAL
THE SUPERIOR PERSON'S GUIDE TO EVERYDAY IRRITATIONS
GIFTING RIGHT

Retail $5.95
LOVE DAT CAT
CRINKLED 'N' WRINKLED
SIGNS YOU'RE A GOLF ADDICT
SMART COMEBACKS FOR STUPID QUESTIONS
YIKES! IT'S ANOTHER BIRTHDAY
SEX IS A GAME
SEX AND YOUR STARS
SIGNS YOUR SEX LIFE IS DEAD
40 AND HOLDING YOUR OWN
50 AND HOLDING YOUR OWN
MALE BASHING: WOMEN'S FAVORITE PASTIME

THINGS YOU CAN DO WITH A USELESS MAN
MORE THINGS YOU CAN DO WITH A USELESS MAN
THE WORLD'S GREATEST PUT-DOWN LINES
LITTLE INSTRUCTION BOOK OF THE RICH & FAMOUS
WELCOME TO YOUR MIDLIFE CRISIS
GETTING EVEN WITH THE ANSWERING MACHINE
ARE YOU A SPORTS NUT?
MEN ARE PIGS / WOMEN ARE BITCHES
ARE WE DYSFUNCTIONAL YET?
TECHNOLOGY BYTES!
50 WAYS TO HUSTLE YOUR FRIENDS ($5.99)
HORMONES FROM HELL
HUSBANDS FROM HELL
KILLER BRAS & Other Hazards Of The 50's
IT'S BETTER TO BE OVER THE HILL THAN UNDER IT
HOW TO REALLY PARTY!!!
WORK SUCKS!
THE PEOPLE WATCHER'S FIELD GUIDE
THE UNOFFICIAL WOMEN'S DIVORCE GUIDE
THE ABSOLUTE LAST CHANCE DIET BOOK
FOR MEN ONLY (How To Survive Marriage)
THE UGLY TRUTH ABOUT MEN
NEVER A DULL CARD
RED HOT MONOGAMY (In Just 60 Seconds A Day) ($6.95)
HOW TO SURVIVE A JEWISH MOTHER ($6.95)
WHY MEN DON'T HAVE A CLUE ($7.99)
LADIES, START YOUR ENGINES! ($7.99)

Retail $3.95
NO HANG-UPS
NO HANG-UPS II
NO HANG-UPS III
HOW TO SUCCEED IN SINGLES BARS
HOW TO GET EVEN WITH YOUR EXES
TOTALLY OUTRAGEOUS BUMPER-SNICKERS ($2.95)

NO HANG-UPS – CASSETTES Retail $4.98
Vol. I:	GENERAL MESSAGES (Female)
Vol. I:	GENERAL MESSAGES (Male)
Vol. II:	BUSINESS MESSAGES (Female)
Vol. II:	BUSINESS MESSAGES (Male)
Vol. III:	'R' RATED MESSAGES (Female)
Vol. III:	'R' RATED MESSAGES (Male)
Vol. IV:	SOUND EFFECTS ONLY
Vol. V:	CELEBRI-TEASE